# The Power to Get Wealth: No Money Required

By Keith Douglas

All scripture quotations are taken from the Old King James Version of the Bible.
All dictionary definitions are taken from Dictionary.com Copyright 2011

The Power to Get Wealth: No Money Required

ISBN-13: 978-0615538167
ISBN-10: 0615538169


P.O. Box 11611
Beverly Hills, CA 90213

Published by Andy Roy Publishing, Inc.
P.O. Box 11611
Beverly Hills, CA 90213

# CONTENTS

# PREFACE

This book is geared FIRST and foremost to the homeless, helpless and disenfranchised. However, it is also for business professionals, entrepreneurs and especially for Spiritual people and lovers of Jesus Christ. Therefore, it is for everyone. (I refer to the bible as a reference because it has been my source of guidance and inspiration. However, this book is not based on religion but on spiritual principles.)

I was inspired to write this book based on the spiritual guidance I obtained through my trials, tribulations and life experience. (Following this guidance has resulted in my success.) I am the sixth child of eight: seven boys and one girl. My mother is amazing. She raised all of us to become productive. In my early childhood I unknowingly suffered from a learning disability known as dyslexia. This disability caused me to read things backwards. I did not want anyone to know about this disability. I was ashamed and didn't understand it at the time. When the teacher said things to the class, I retained every word and clearly understood what she was talking about but was unable to express myself on paper.

So, being embarrassed about my condition, I would make up any reason to leave the classroom. When I was in class, I'd laugh out loud, horse-play around and use excuses to leave such as being sick or having to go to the restroom. This behavior resulted in me being kicked out of all elementary and junior high schools and being labeled as a "troubled youth".

Not wanting to face my disability, I chose to hang out with other "troubled youth". They became my family. They admired me and looked up to me as a leader and someone that they could talk to. Despite of the circumstances, I had it in me to inspire all of them who were around me at the time to get out of gangs and stop stealing. One day my mother wanted me to read directions for her that someone else had written. To her dismay, I read everything backwards. That is when she discovered there was a problem. I received professional help for my condition. Although I am sometimes challenged with it, I have overcome my disability.

As a child I was always attracted to great leaders, speeches, bible scriptures and God's word. I have been blessed with a gift of interpretation of God's word and revelation. I have used this gift as well as my life experience to rise from a below average student to a premier entrepreneur. My interpersonal skills helped me elevate rapidly in many fields including management, marketing, public relations and telecommunications. I am currently a successful Entrepreneur, CEO and President of two notable music companies.

I have always been inspired to write a book from my passion for the homeless, the helpless and troubled individuals. I have combined my life experience and extensive biblical studies to help unlock and free people from *religion* which is man-made, and understand spiritual principles such as faith, confidence, self-esteem, health and wealth. I live by these principles and have shared them with many others who have benefited tremendously.

I began to write this book because of countless phone calls, meetings, seminars and interactions requesting my spiritual advice. So I did what God's word told me to do. **Habakkuk 2:2-3 "And the LORD answered me, and said, Write the vision, and make it plain upon tables, that he may run that readeth it. For the vision is yet for an appointed time, but at the end it shall speak, and not lie: though it tarry, wait for it; because it will surely come, it will not tarry."**

This book is easy to read and includes simple principles and daily practices:

*-Understanding the Natural vs. the Supernatural*
*-The Seen vs. the Unseen*
*-Faith vs. Fear*

*-Understanding the true meaning of Wealth and the Power to move in God's kingdom effectively.*

I hope and pray that everyone who reads this book will receive the revelation of God's word and become eternally free.

God Bless
Keith Douglas

THE POWER TO GET WEALTH: NO MONEY REQUIRED

**IS THIS REALLY WEALTH?**

# Chapter One

## Fiction or Non Fiction (The Misperception of Wealth)

Many people in the world today have the wrong understanding of what wealth truly means. Therefore, they have no idea of what wealth is or how to become wealthy. We live in a natural world full of material things such as homes, cars, jewelry and money. As children, we learn about wealth through television and our perception of entertainers, athletes etc.

Many of us are taught by our parents to go to school, learn as much as we can and get as much as we can. We follow this advice not knowing that all of the above has nothing to do with wealth. You can live in a one-bedroom apartment, or you can live in your car. No matter what your situation may be you can still be wealthy. This may sound a little crazy to the natural thinker.

**1 Corinthians 2:14 "But the natural man receiveth not the things of the Spirit of God: for they are foolishness unto him: neither can he know them, because they are spiritually discerned.**" In order to understand the full effect of wealth you must believe in the natural as well as the supernatural. ***Natural*** means ***within your 'own ability'***.

For example, all of us are born with a gift in some shape or form but it is up to us to discover our gifts. ***Supernatural*** means ***outside of your own ability***. In order for the supernatural to work, we must let go and let God. **Philippians 2:5 "Christ said Let <u>this</u> mind be in you, which was also in Jesus Christ."** This is the spiritual mind through which we can do all things. This means that NOTHING is impossible!

In the natural mind you are limited to the flesh. **John 3:6 "That which is born of the flesh is flesh; and that which is born of the Spirit is spirit."** You see the flesh is weak but the spirit is willing *(action verb).* It will work if you work it. So, I guess you are wondering by now what is the true meaning of wealth. It is so simple. The true meaning of ***wealth is all <u>needs</u> met***. For example, if you do live in that one-bedroom apartment, have everything you need, and are happy, you are wealthy.

The misperception that wealth is based upon how many things we have is a trick from Satan. He has no power. We give him power! We see so many successful entertainers, sports figures, lawyers and doctors in the media with many scandals and virtually no peace. It appears that they have everything but in actuality they do not.

If you don't have the spirit and a Christ-like mind you don't have anything but things. Things will never fulfill our true desires or needs. It is no different from an alcoholic who depends on a drink to soothe them, instead of correcting what's haunting them deep down inside. It's just a temporary fix that will never fulfill the desire of the human being.

Now that we have the proper understanding of what wealth is, let's start off on the right foot and reverse the curse. I'm not suggesting that you should not have great things or many things. Christ said in **John 10:10 "... I come that they might have life and that they might have it more abundantly."** The truth of the matter is that most of us have many things but still have no peace in our lives. We are one pay check away from being homeless. We are strapped down with credit cards and debt and smile while we are really crying inside.

Once we begin to understand that true wealth is all *needs met,* we can live life more comfortably without having a champagne taste with a beer budget. By following the principles in this book, you will be able to obtain the desires of your heart and have the things that you've always dreamed of. You will experience peace, happiness and mind over matter, not matter over mind.

In order to reverse the curse, you must first be honest with yourself and be willing to evaluate where you are in your life. Do you have a lot of things and no peace? I advise you to take a step back and take an honest look at your condition. Begin to seek happiness through life in general. Be thankful for the little things such as waking up, having food to eat, having a place to lay your head, friends, family and job.

If you have a lot of things and no happiness, it's never too late to get it together. Each day you can correct one thing at a time and eventually things will turn around. Your life will transform supernaturally by following the principles of God's word which I will disclose further in the book.

So now if you understand the principles that have been expressed to you begin to say to yourself – My name is *(your name)* and I am WEALTHY! Remember whatever you focus on it expands. If you focus on negativity it expands; if you focus on positivity it expands. So stay motivated, healthy and wealthy.

KEITH DOUGLAS

**DO YOU KNOW SELF?**

## Chapter Two

# SELF WORTH = WEALTH

In the first chapter, we got a clear understanding that wealth is – all needs met. In this chapter, we will learn how to expand our wealth and self worth. We will also see how feeling wealthy attracts wealth. Once you are free from the misperception about true wealth, you will begin to see that your source is not in the world outside, but within you.

The disciples asked Christ 'Good Master, how can we see the kingdom?' He replied, "None is good but God, the kingdom is within you." Everything you need as a human being is inside of you. **John 4:24 "God is Spirit and they that worship him must worship him in spirit and truth."**

Once you know yourself you can do the unimaginable. When we look outside of self, we are limited to what we see. This is why the word instructs us to walk by faith and not by sight. The natural man and woman believe it's impossible to walk without seeing where they're going. Yet once you understand the spirit you will understand that you can see beyond your own eyes.

When you get up to walk do you look at your legs? We expect our legs to do the walking for us without looking down; that's true faith. So let's get back to wealth and self worth. It is very important that you become a reader of the word because the word tells us that in the beginning was the word and the word was with God and the word was God.

The more knowledge, wisdom and skills you acquire, the more you expand your self-worth. The more you know spiritually, physically and intellectually, the more you're worth.

When we commit ourselves to learning, doing, helping and loving as much as we can, we become servants of the most high. **Romans 12:1 "I beseech you therefore, brethren, by the mercies of God, that ye present your bodies a living sacrifice, holy, acceptable unto God, which is your reasonable service.**" The word once again becomes true: Give and it shall be given unto you, press down shaken up and running over.

God's principles will never fail, so the more we love, give, help, tithe, the more we build our self-worth. These principles lead to overflow in our lives. We began to have more than enough and are able to help others. That's our service. The word tells us in **Psalms 1:3, "And he shall be like a tree planted by the rivers of water, that bringeth forth his fruit in his season; his leaf also shall not wither; and whatsoever he doeth shall prosper."** It is no different than having a penny in your pocket versus a quarter. You know that the quarter is worth more.

Thus, it is important to find ways to increase our confidence and self-esteem. Without confidence and high self-esteem we cannot realize our true worth. The enemy comes to steal, kill and destroy. For example if he steals your self -esteem he kills your dream.

If he kills your dreams, he destroys you.

In today's world things are moving so fast and there's so much to keep us distracted. The enemy tries to keep us busy because an idle mind is the devil's workshop. If you look outside more than you look within, you will be tricked every time. We spend more time doing someone else's business than we do our own.

Your job is temporary. Your goals and dreams are eternal. Thus, it is imperative that we take time out to center ourselves through meditation, prayer and relaxation. The word tells us in **Isaiah 26:3 "Thou wilt keep him in perfect peace, whose mind is stayed on thee: because he trusteth in thee.**" It is important to speak positive things all day sometimes. Begin to say to yourself things like:

**"I can do all things through Christ who strengthens me"**

**"I'm more than a Conqueror"**
**"I'm the head and not the tail"**
**"I will lend and not borrow"**

Positive thinking is a must. Surround yourself with positive thinkers. If you are the smartest person in your circle you're not that smart at all. Always look for someone who is smarter, knows more and is doing more so you can elevate your self-worth. The more you elevate your self-worth, the more you can obtain all the things you desire and have them for as long as you like. It becomes a lifestyle that literally attracts wealth.

You will become a light in a world of darkness and everyone will be attracted to you because of what shines from inside of you. Always remember as God's word tells us in **1 John 4:4 "Greater is he that is in you than he that is in the world."** Once we gain power over our natural selves and begin to operate in the supernatural, we begin to understand how to operate in God's kingdom and how to overcome any obstacles that we encounter.

**Matthew 17:20 "... If ye have faith as a grain of mustard seed, ye shall say unto this mountain, Remove hence to yonder place; and it shall remove; and nothing shall be impossible unto you."** The natural mind may think of a literal mountain. The spiritual mind that thinks obstacle is correct. The word also tells us that we can speak to the mountain/obstacle and say **"Be cast into the sea and it will be remembered no more."**

No matter what obstacle we may have, we can overcome it if we keep speaking to it positively. We will get through it, get over it and come out with more strength and more power. These are some of the primary principles of self-worth which equals wealth. **3 John 1:2 "Beloved, I wish above all things that thou mayest prosper and be in good health, even as thy soul prospereth."**

As you begin to follow all of the above principles and stay in God's word, you will begin to have more strength and more revelation. The best feeling in life is to have true understanding. **Revelation** causes **Resurrection**. This leads to a **Miracle** mind set which leads to **Expectation**.

**Romans 4:17**, **"...calleth those things which be not as though they were."** This is mind over matter not matter over mind. Expectation becomes a mind set of expecting good things all the time. Even when we're faced with trials and tribulations we still expect the best. **Romans 8:28, "And we know that all things work together for good to them that love God, to them who are the called according**

**to his purpose.**" So even in trials we look for the blessing.

For example, there was a young man who was looking forward to getting his first car. His parents eventually bought the car for him. He kept the car immaculate. He washed and shined it every week. He was careful about who drove in it and would never let anyone drive. He literally treated that car like it was his everything.

One day he was driving down the road and was struck by a drunk driver. The car was totally demolished. The firemen freed him from the wrecked car. Upon getting to the hospital with virtually no injuries and just a scratch on his forehead, he was devastated about the loss of the car. The young man totally missed the blessing in this instance. Although his car was totaled, he came out of the accident with just a scratch.

What he didn't realize is that things can be replaced and the blessing was that he was not injured. The spiritual mind-set will overcome anything and high self-worth will build confidence and character in any situation. Always remember your self-worth = wealth.

THE POWER TO GET WEALTH: NO MONEY REQUIRED

**DON'T GIVE UP**

## Chapter Three

# FAITH

*Faith*. We commonly hear this word more than usual. It's a buzz word in our society today. However, you can ask ten different people what faith is and you will get ten different answers. My mission is to give you a clear in-depth understanding of faith.

Faith is the key to unlocking your gateway to success and spiritual understanding. In order to properly understand faith we must once again look at it in both the natural and the spiritual contexts. **Hebrews 11:6 "But**

**without faith it is impossible to please him: for he that cometh to God must believe that he is, and that he is a rewarder of them that diligently seek him."**

The word ***impossible*** is a strong word. According to the dictionary ***impossible*** means ***not possible; unable to be, exist or happen***. Now we know if we do not have or understand faith, it inhibits us from excelling or accomplishing anything in the natural or spiritual realm. Most people use faith everyday unconsciously. The enemy (Satan) loves this because when we use it unconsciously it's tied to the flesh and not to the spirit. Therefore, although we are using it every day, we stay in the same position whether it is in our dreams, goals or job positions.

So what exactly is faith? **Hebrews 11:1 "Now faith is the substance of**

**things hoped for, the evidence of things not seen.**" Let's break this down. The word **_now_** is an adverb meaning *at the present time or moment.* The word **substance** is a noun which means ***that of which a thing consists; physical matter or material.***

The word **things** is a noun meaning ***a material object without life or consciousness; an inanimate object.*** The word **hoped** is a verb meaning ***the feeling that what is wanted can be had or that events will turn out for the best.*** The word **evidence** is a noun which means ***that which tends to prove or disprove something; ground for belief; proof.*** And lastly, the word **seen** is a verb and means ***to perceive with the eyes; look at***.

Now that we have a proper breakdown lets put it together. Faith is **NOW**. Not tomorrow or not next week, but NOW. Faith is the substance of things (cars, homes, jewelry, money, etc.) hoped for (desires, needs, wants, expectations). Faith is the evidence of things not seen (belief, faith and vision). **Romans 4:17 "... calleth those things which be not as though they were."**

We must believe and receive what we desire in advance. It is very important that you take mental photographs of the things that you desire so you can exercise your faith towards getting them.

**2 Corinthians 5:7 "For we walk by faith, not by sight."** We are limited by what we see, however; what we see is tied to the flesh. There is no limit to what we believe. **Matthew 26:41 "Watch and pray, that ye enter not into temptation: the spirit indeed is willing, but the flesh is weak."** The spirit is tied to your faith. What we see is tied to our flesh. Most people use faith according to their flesh and they are limited to only natural things and not spiritual things.

For example, we work on our jobs for a whole year without missing a day. It takes faith to accomplish this. We set our minds on having perfect attendance and accomplish it. However, the same person that never misses a day on their job can barely survive each month because their job doesn't pay them enough.

They complain day in and day out about getting a better job but refuse to use that same faith to get a better job. Notice, they could only see where they were now versus believe where they could be because they used their faith in the natural way and not in a spiritual way.

The reason I'm giving you this example, is because we use our faith everyday unconsciously and are reluctant to use our faith correctly. I'll be giving you more examples throughout this chapter on using your faith properly.

**Romans 10:17, "Faith cometh by hearing and hearing by the word of God**." We also see that faith also comes by hearing. It is extremely important that you are cautious about what you hear and listen to as well as what people tell you and what you are telling yourself. Notice, we have two ears and one mouth. Most people talk more with one mouth and listen less with two ears.

Remember the flesh is weak and the spirit is willing which means the spirit will work if you work it. If you don't read the word you will never know how to use the word. If someone tells you something or whispers something to you and it does not line up with the word of God it is not for you. So, hearing the right things sets us up to use our faith properly. Remember words are very important.

**Matthew 4:4 "Man shall not live by bread alone, but by every word that proceedeth out of the mouth of God."**

This is extremely important. **John 1:1 "In the beginning was the Word, and the Word was with God, and the Word was God."** Most people say they believe and they have faith, but really don't understand how faith works. You can't have true faith without knowing God's word. Most people have faith in their flesh, not faith in their spirit. **John 4:24 "God is a Spirit: and they that worship him must worship him in spirit and in truth."**

*Using faith to deal with your problems and challenges.*

Faith is not only used for manifesting our desires. It's also used to sustain us during trials and tribulations. Most people have faith as long as everything is going okay in their lives. However, once trials hit them, they go from being on top of a hill to being deep in the valley. Satan (the enemy) loves to test our faith through our trials and tribulations.

It is necessary to establish the truth so when we go through things, God can elevate our faith. Never forget there are only two forces in this world: faith and fear. **2 Chronicles 20:15 "....for the battle is not yours, but God's."** So when trouble comes it is our job as believers to use our faith, not try to fight our own battles or trials.

True faith lifts up a standard inside of us and drives Satan away. **Matthew 17:20 "And Jesus said unto them, Because of your unbelief: for verily I say unto you, If ye have faith as a grain of mustard seed, ye shall say unto this mountain, Remove hence to yonder place; and it shall**

**remove; and nothing shall be impossible unto you.**" Let me elaborate. You can barely see a mustard seed because it is so small to the natural eye but God did not limit us to just a mustard seed. Why don't we have the faith the size of a mountain?

**Mountains** are just obstacles in our lives. When we truly understand faith we can speak to any obstacle and get over it with our faith. It is very important that when we have trials and tribulations in our lives we continue to use our faith. By speaking God's word over and over again to our mountains/obstacles, we will receive our breakthroughs.

Remember the race is not given to the fast or the swift, but is given to the one who endures until the end. We must have patience during challenging times, because God may not come when we want him to come but he will come on time. Also, obedience is greater than sacrifice. So during challenging time, we must be obedient. **Isaiah 40:31 "But they that wait upon the Lord shall renew their strength; they shall mount up with wings as eagles; they shall run, and not be weary; and they shall walk, and not faint."**

*Faith vs. Fear*

Now that we have a clear understanding of faith, let's deal with the consequences of not having faith. **Hebrews 11:6 "But without faith it is impossible to please him: for he that cometh to God must believe that he is, and that he is a rewarder of them that diligently seek him."** Most people use their faith every day unconsciously to satisfy their flesh. If they used their faith correctly, there would be no limits in their life.

When we use faith incorrectly we make ourselves vulnerable to the enemy. The consequences of not using faith correctly are **fear, pain, doubt, low self-esteem, depression, anxiety, stress, frustration, unhappiness and lack of peace.** Now let's get a proper understanding of fear. According to the dictionary ***fear*** is a noun which means ***a distressing emotion aroused by impending danger, evil, pain, etc., whether the threat is real or imagined; the feeling or condition of being afraid***.

Notice the definition states whether the threat of fear is real or imagined. **2 Timothy 1:7 "For God hath not given us the spirit of fear; but of power, and of love, and of a sound mind."** Here's my definition of fear – **False Emotions Appearing to be Real,** which spells **FEAR**. The enemy doesn't have any power. We give him power. Fear limits us from speaking the truth, elevating in life, examining ourselves and many other things. Our protection against fear as believers is faith and using the word of God. I would advise all believers to study the scriptures on fear.

Some of my favorites are **Hebrews 13:5-6**, **Ephesians 6:10-18**, **2 Corinthians 7:1**, **Proverbs 3:5-7** and **Psalms 34:5**. Remember the word tells us in **1 John 4:18 "There is no fear in love; but perfect love casteth out fear: because fear hath torment. He that feareth is not made perfect in love."** You see the more you get into God's word, the more power and strength you receive.

For example, if someone had a bad cold and did not treat it, it could potentially turn into pneumonia and ultimately death. If the same person treated the cold with proper medicine and rest, they would have recovered. It is very important to identify areas in our lives where we are weak and fall short. If we do not face our weaknesses or fears we will not get stronger.

Always remember whatever you focus your mind on it expands. For example, if you focus your mind on faith it expands. If you focus your mind on fear it also expands, but once your faith is solid as a rock fear begins to fear you. Choose faith not fear.

THE POWER TO GET WEALTH: NO MONEY REQUIRED

**NO LIMITS**

## Chapter Four

# KINGDOM THINKING

Many people refer to a kingdom as a place where a king or a queen resides, a state or government. A king is usually a ruler and whatever he (king/queen) decrees or declares becomes law. In this chapter it is very critical that you keep an open mind because we will be dealing with two natures; the natural and the supernatural. **The word *natural*, meaning *within your ability*** and ***Supernatural*, *meaning outside of your ability*. The word**

**kingdom is also referred to in the bible as the '*kingdom of God*'.** According to the dictionary the word ***kingdom*** means ***the domain over which the spiritual sovereignty of God or Christ extends, whether in heaven or on earth.***

In this chapter, we will be focusing on kingdom thinking. In order to understand kingdom thinking, you must operate in the spirit and not the flesh. **Proverbs 23:7 "For as he thinketh in his heart, so is he...."** Also, the scripture tells us in **Philippians 2:5 "Let this mind be in you, which was also in Christ Jesus."** Notice, the scripture refers to the mind of Christ, not your mind. Jesus was his name. Christ wasn't his last name but Christ was given to him by God. ***Christ*** means ***'one anointed with the power to destroy the wicked'***.

In order to operate in kingdom thinking, you must have a Christ-like mind. This is very important because without a Christ-like mind you will operate in self-will which is tied to your flesh. **Romans 12:2 "And be not conformed to this world: but be ye transformed by the renewing of your mind, that ye may prove what is that good, and acceptable, and perfect, will of God."** A conformed mind set is the enemy of a kingdom mindset because the kingdom mindset is transformed.

When we think like a king or a queen, this requires high esteem as well as excellence. Whatever a king or a queen decrees it becomes the law of the land. Some may ask "How can I renew my mind?" Easy! We renew our minds by accepting the word of God and rejecting fear, doubt, negativity and worldly things. Also by praying, fasting, studying, meditating, loving and serving. **2 Corinthians 10:5 "...and bringing into captivity every**

**thought to the obedience of Christ..."** So, when we get ideas or make decisions we must examine our thoughts and make sure that they line up with the word of God. If it does not, it is not of a Christ-like mind.

For example, if you wanted to write someone an important letter you would examine that letter first before you sent it. It is very important that we keep our minds on the word of God in order to stay strong in God. **Isaiah 26:3 "Thou wilt keep him in perfect peace, whose mind is stayed on thee: because he trusteth in thee."** Notice that when we keep our minds on God, we experience peace in our lives. Our peace begins to decrease when we encounter worldly challenges, however, with practice, we can be in the world and not of the world.

Kingdom people stand out like lights in a world of darkness. People look at us differently. We are treated differently. Favor is given to us. We are a very peculiar people. When people say something can't be done, we say we can. When life brings us trials and tribulations we stand on the word because we know God cannot lie. This is easier said than done.

You must train yourself. Yet, the more you practice, the more Anointing and Power you will receive. Soon it will become second nature to think positive and use wisdom as keys to the kingdom. Once you receive the keys, doors will be unlocked that no man can shut because God has opened them. **Romans 8:31 "What shall we then say to these things? If God be for us, who can be against us?"**

*Operating in the kingdom*

Now that we have established kingdom thinking, it's time for us to put our thoughts to work by operating in the kingdom and activating God's word. **Luke 17:21 "Neither shall they say, Lo here! or, lo there! for, behold, the kingdom of God is within you."** It is very important that we look within ourselves and not out because everything we need is already in us. The word says in **Revelations 3:20, "Behold, I stand at the door, and knock: if any man hear my voice, and open the door, I will come in to him, and will sup with him, and he with me."**

Once we know who we are and whose we are, the enemy has no power over us. We press forward regardless of what the circumstances or situation may be. We praise God in the good times and the so-called bad times because as **Romans 8:28 tells us "And we know that all things work together for good to them that**

**love God, to them who are the called according to his purpose."**

Once we understand that trials and tribulations are necessary to establish the truth, we accept that life comes with challenges. Sometimes in order for God to elevate us he must test us but the battle is not ours, it is the Lord's. **Galatians 6:9 "And let us not be weary in well doing: for in due season we shall reap, if we faint not."** So when we let go and let God, we begin to grow and elevate into maturity.

Just like there are seasons in the world, there are seasons in our lives. So when you are going through trials, remember the bigger the trial, the bigger the blessing! The enemy wants you to miss your blessing. **John 10:10 tells us, "The thief cometh not, but for to <u>steal</u>, and to <u>kill</u>, and to <u>destroy</u>: I am come that they might**

**have life, and that they might have it more abundantly."**

God's purpose for us is elevation and in order for us to grow he must stretch us and shape us. God never squeezes us; he stretches us to widen our territory. The natural man and the natural woman do not understand this. That's why they keep going in circles in their lives. It's the same conversations, the same routines and the same problems year in and year out. They settle and give in to the enemy's plan.

The enemy doesn't care if we know the word; he knows the word too. We defeat him when we act on the word. As long as he can keep us standing still in the kingdom he is not threatened. **Matthew 11:12 "And from the days of John the Baptist until now the kingdom of heaven suffereth violence, and the violent take it by force."** In order for us to operate effectively in the kingdom we must put

on the full armor of God because we
are at war. **Ephesians 6:11-17 "Put
on the whole armour of God, that ye
may be able to stand against the
wiles of the devil.**
12For **we wrestle not against
flesh and blood, but against
principalities, against powers,
against the rulers of the darkness
of this world, against spiritual
wickedness in high places.**
13**Wherefore take unto you the
whole armour of God, that ye may
be able to withstand in the evil day,
and having done all, to stand.**
14**Stand therefore, having your
loins girt about with truth, and
having on the breastplate of
righteousness;**
15**And your feet shod with the
preparation of the gospel of peace;**
16**Above all, taking the shield of
faith, wherewith ye shall be able to**

**quench all the fiery darts of the wicked.**

**17 And take the helmet of salvation, and the sword of the Spirit, which is the word of God..."**

Most of us wake up in the morning defeated. We forget to pray, meditate and study. When we forget to bless our day we are vulnerable to Satan's plans. He desires for us not to be protected and when we are not protected he attacks us. Most of us are scared when we hear the word 'war' but this war that we're in is the best war we could be in because in this war we are not required to battle or fight. God does it for us!

For example, you get up in the morning and forget to pray and put on the armor of God. You get to work and a customer tells you something that you didn't like. You lose control and tell the customer off. The result of losing control costs you your job. This could have been handled a totally different way if you would have had on the armor of God. What the customer said wouldn't have bothered you. **Proverbs 16:18 "Pride goeth before destruction, and an haughty spirit before a fall."**

The enemy attacks us in the kingdom where we are weak so it is important that we challenge ourselves in areas where we are weak. Any area where we are challenged is the area where God wants to bless and elevate us. Once we are mature in God, we are ready to operate in the kingdom. **Matthew 6:33 "But seek ye first the kingdom of God, and his righteousness; and all these things shall be added unto you."**

Righteousness doesn't mean we're perfect, it means right standing with God and maturity. Once we are matured, God knows that we can endure anything and we are ready to accept the blessings he has in store for us.

Let's break this down. The word ***Kingdom*** according to the dictionary means ***the domain over which the spiritual sovereignty of God or Christ extends, whether in heaven or on earth.*** The disciples asked Christ, "How can we see the kingdom?" He told them "None is good but God, the kingdom is within you." So now we see the kingdom is within us. The word tells us but seek ye first the kingdom of God.

Now according to the dictionary the word ***righteousness*** means ***the quality or state of being righteous; holiness; purity; uprightness; rectitude.*** So when we know whose we are and who we are in Christ Jesus, we are the righteousness of God. Once we are mature, then all these things shall be added unto us. The word ***maturity*** according to the dictionary means ***full development or perfected condition.***

Lack in your life, is due to lack of maturity in that area. God will bless you in every area where you are mature. If you're immature in your finances God will not bless you financially. If you're immature in your marriage, your marriage will not grow. Most Christians are immature; that's why we are on a mountaintop one day and in a valley the next day.

Let's put all of this into order.

1) Seek God first, because the kingdom is within you not outside of you.

2) Study the word; know Christ; get maturity and right standing with God.

3) Once you apply the first two principles, then all of these things shall be added unto you: belief, faith, peace, wealth and health.

If we examine our lives, we will find that every area where we're not mature will be reflected in areas of our lives where we are lacking in. Once we are mature in that area, there will no longer be lack. God can now work through us and for us.

Our attitudes determine our altitudes. Kingdom thinking requires peace, happiness, joy and love. When we get confused, it is because the enemy is trying to set us off course because peace is the absence of confusion and confusion is the absence of peace. **Nehemiah 8:10 "...for this day is holy unto our LORD: neither be ye sorry; for the joy of the LORD is your strength."**

Now that you know what kingdom thinking is and how to operate in kingdom thinking, I hope that you will put these principles to work and enjoy the life that God intended for his children, God Bless.

KEITH DOUGLAS

**DREAM**

# Chapter Five

# VISION

Vision is essential to success. It opens doors that no man can shut because they come directly from God. In this chapter, we will distinguish vision from dreams and get a proper understanding of how to use vision correctly.

According to the dictionary the word ***Vision*** means ***'the act or power of anticipating that which will or may come to be: prophetic vision; the vision of an entrepreneur.'***

**Proverbs 29:18** states **"Where there is no Vision, the people perish, but he that keepeth the law, happy is he."**

Notice the word says 'the people perish'. The word perish is a strong word. God didn't say where there is no prayer or faith or belief the people perish. He said where there is no vision, the people perish. According to the dictionary, the word ***perish*** *means* ***to suffer spiritual death.***

When we fail to understand vision whether conscious or unconscious, we suffer spiritual death. We cannot hear God speaking to us in the spirit or see God's vision because of our lack of obedience in following his instructions. Abraham was given his name (which means the friend of God) by the Lord. He received many visions.

**Genesis 15:1** states **"After these things the word of the LORD came unto Abram in a vision, saying,**

**Fear not, Abram: I am thy shield, and thy exceeding great reward.**" Vision is the manuscript for our lives. **Psalm 37:23** says, "**The steps of a good man are ordered by the LORD: and he delighteth in his way.**" How will you know your steps are ordered by the Lord, unless you have communication with God or Spirit?

**John 4:24 states "God is Spirit and they that worship him must worship him in spirit and truth**." There's a big difference between a vision and a dream. Dreams don't always come true but visions will always come true. *According to the dictionary, the word* ***dream*** *means* ***a succession of images, thoughts, or emotions passing through the mind during sleep.***

Notice that vision is a conscious state and dreams are an unconscious state. It is important to understand the difference between the natural and the supernatural. Dreamers operate in a natural state of mind. Visionaries operate in a Supernatural state of mind.

**Habakkuk 2:2-3 "And the Lord answered me and said write the Vision and make it plain upon tables that he may run that readeth it for the vision is yet for an appointed time but at the end it shall speak and not lie; though it may tarry, wait for it because it will surely come; it will not tarry."**

Notice the scripture said "And the Lord answered me." The Lord couldn't have answered him unless he asked for something. For instance, when you pray and ask God for something you expect to receive an answer whether through a person, an experience or an accomplishment. Sometimes our prayers may not get answered. Vision is important because when we pray and ask God for something whether it be for ourselves or others, God will always give us an answer through people, signs and revelation.

But if we don't take heed to the signs or instructions that God gives us, we will miss the mark. Whenever God gives you a vision it's extremely important to write it down no matter what time of day it is. Be obedient and write down what God reveals to you. Make sure you don't tell anyone what God told you in your vision. The word says "He that readeth it may run with it." So if you tell someone your vision, they can take it and benefit from it.

It happens every day. For instance Pam, an aspiring singer, received a vision to write a song called "Never Give Up." She called her friend and told her about this new song she had come up with. She even sung the lyrics to her so called friend. A couple years later she heard her song on the radio and was blown away. She was very dismayed and hurt because she had only told her friend. She never wrote down the lyrics or copyrighted the song and eventually the song became a number one hit.

So, when you receive a vision, don't hesitate or procrastinate and don't add to it or take away from it. Make it plain. When God gives you a vision or instructions it is no different than Moses receiving the Commandments. It becomes law. Do not question if it will happen. It has to happen.

The reason you have to write it down quickly is because it's not coming from you, it's coming from God. You must be obedient. The word tells us that the vision is yet for an appointed time. Natural people fail to hear the word of God through vision, so they miss the answer to their prayers and they don't receive their inheritance.

**Psalm 51:5 "Behold, I was shapen in iniquity; and in sin did my mother conceive me."** You can't be shaped unless there is a shaper and the shaper is the enemy. So, we must reverse the curse. Notice, that when kids come into the world, they are innocent. They have such great promise but as they get older their innocence begins to fade. You're probably wondering why? It's because they enter into a world of sin. We should be in the world but not of the world.

Here's an example. Most little girls have diaries. Their diaries consist of their hopes, their dreams and daily activities but as they get older they put their diaries away. This is a big mistake, because those diaries were filled with so many visions, hopes, inspirations and dreams.

I would advise every woman to go back and find your diary because it contains so much valuable information. Never feel as though you are too old to have a diary. Everyone should have a vision book or a journal. Think about it, where would we be if the prophets did not obey God and write their vision in the book from Genesis to Revelations? We would be lost. Everyone should have a book. When God gives us a vision we have something to look forward to and the more we hearken to his voice and obey the more he will communicate with his children.

**Joel 2:28 "...your old men shall dream dreams; your young men shall see visions."** I would advise all parents to encourage their kids to keep on believing, dreaming and hoping because the kids are our future. Now, begin to write your vision.

## MY VISION BOOK

# MY VISION BOOK

## MY VISION BOOK

## MY VISION BOOK

THE POWER TO GET WEALTH: NO MONEY REQUIRED

**SEED**

## Chapter Six

# NO MONEY DOWN

This chapter is one of my most important chapters. It is extremely important that you keep an open mind by using the principles and tools in previous chapters along with understanding the natural vs. the supernatural. No money down means exactly that. No exceptions. Without belief and faith you will not be able to activate these principles. We should never use the word spend.

According to the dictionary, the word ***spend*** means ***to throw away or to squander.*** We should always use the word 'invest'. According to the dictionary, the word **invest** means **to use, give, or devote (time, talent, etc.), as for a purpose or to achieve something.** Investing time in people who are not going anywhere will always set you back. Always look for people who are going places and doing more.

No money down is something we love to hear in the natural world. When we hear that we can get anything for no money down, it gets our attention. In the natural world things are built on credit and fiscal scores. This means if you have bad credit you get high interest rates or maybe nothing at all. If you have good credit you can get anything.

Notice things are based on scores and not on how much money, possessions or collateral one may have. For example, a doctor that makes a lot of money in his practice may also have an extremely high over head: school loans, expenses, or employee payroll. He could be in a position where although he's making a lot of money, he can't get any credit or finance or lease a car because of too much overhead.

However, a recent college graduate with a menial job and little money can get a car loan quicker than a doctor. Just because one may have a lot of things in this world, that doesn't mean that they are any better than the person who has very little.

As a matter of fact, most people that have a lot of things in life are very unhappy because they find peace in things rather than inside of themselves. The enemy's number one goal is to get you looking outside of yourself versus inside of yourself.

Notice that the things you receive in the world are temporary and the things you get from God are permanent. This is why we say according to the word in **Romans 4:17 "...and calleth those things which be not as though they were."** In order to call something that isn't, you must have belief and power. The natural man and woman go according to what they see and not what the word tells them.

**2 Corinthians 5:7 "For we walk by faith and not by sight."** That scripture is used loosely in the body of Christ. Most of us say it but really don't believe it. Because if we really believed it, we would know that judging life according to what we see limits us from what we can truly be.

Now the enemy's main objective is to blind believers with material things. For example, the devil took Christ upon a hill and said to him "If you would bow down to me I will give you all of this world." Christ rejected him and told him to get behind him.

Once we start looking within ourselves and God's spirit, rather than looking outside of ourselves, we begin to develop a relationship with God's word. We begin to realize that our real blessings come from him. We also begin to establish a permanent relationship with God.

Once we establish a relationship with God, we will understand what the word tells us in **Philippians 4:19 "But my God shall supply all your need according to his riches in glory by Christ Jesus."**

**2 Corinthians 8:9 "For ye know the grace of our Lord Jesus Christ, that, though he was rich, yet for your sakes he became poor that ye through his poverty might be rich."**

**Job 36:11 "If they obey and serve him they shall spend their**

**days in prosperity and their years in pleasure."**

**Psalms 112:1-3 "Blessed is the man that feareth the Lord, that delights greatly in his commandments.....Wealth and riches shall be in his house."**

**Deuteronomy 8:18 "You shall remember the Lord your God for it is he who gives you Power to get Wealth. That he may establish his covenant which He swore to your fathers as it is this day."**

**John 10:10 "The thief cometh not but to steal, and to kill, and to destroy. I am come that they might have life, and that they might have it more abundantly."**

**Psalms 35:27 "Let the Lord be magnified who pleasure in prosperity of his servant."**

I guess by now you may be asking yourself why I called this chapter No Money Down. It's simple. When you follow God's principles, God will follow you.

**Mark 11:23-24 "Jesus said, Whoever says to this mountain, 'Be removed and be cast into the sea,' and does not doubt in his heart, but believes that those things he says will come to pass, he will have whatever he says."** Therefore I say to you, whatever things you ask when you pray, believe that you will receive them and you shall have them.

It is very important for the believer to know that their prayers are stronger than their natural ability. In other words, we must let go and let God. When we believe God's word our prayers will be answered. For example, you want a new car.

First, you must identify and claim what you desire. Next, give yourself a plan to get the car. Thirdly, start working your plan and God will do the rest supernaturally. Notice we pay for things but not for belief. When we believe God's word he will give us the provision to obtain the possession.

A woman worked on her job very hard for three years. She saw that there was a new executive position posted. She really wanted to advance in the company. She prayed and believed and asked God to bless her with the position. She applied for the position and received an interview date. She asked several executives in the company what type of things would be required of her to get that position. She then took all of their advice and started preparing herself for the interview. She studied the position and all of its requirements and got herself ready for the interview.

The day of the interview she was among ten candidates. When she was interviewed, the board was so impressed with her answers, personality and knowledge, that they offered her the job right on the spot. Notice that she prayed and believed and took the necessary steps to prepare for the interview.

**James 2:26 "For as the body without the spirit is dead so faith without works is dead also."** If you want God to move, you must move. Notice that she didn't pay any money for this position. She used her belief. If you base all of your trust on money it will become your God. The word doesn't tell us that *money is the root of all evil.* It tells us that *'the love of money is the root of all evil.'* The love of God is all we need.

The more we seek God, the more he will reveal to us wisdom keys to unlock life's doors. The sooner we realize that all of our blessings come from God, the sooner we will begin to rely on God. During times when things get tough in life hold on to his word and promise. God's word can't lie nor return void. That should make it much easier for us because he can't lie and as long as we rely on his word, we can't fail.

Most of us bring fear, doubt, stress and anxiety on ourselves because of the lack of believing and reading God's word. He will not put any more on us than we can bear. This scripture doesn't only apply to trials and tribulations. The natural man and woman thinks affliction only. The spiritual man and woman think correctly. God will not give you more prosperity than you can bear.

Where ever we are matured, God will bless us in that area. If we get things in life before we are ready to handle them, it won't be long before we lose them. Whatever is on the inside of you will manifest on the outside of you. If you think positive and believe, you will be a light in a world of darkness. People will be attracted to your light. Everyone will want to be a part of you. People will believe in you; people will trust you; people will give to you.

**Luke 6:38 "Give and it shall be given unto you; good measure, pressed down, and shaken together, and running over, shall men give into your bosom. For with the same measure that ye mete withal it shall be measured to you again."**

One of the main keys to this chapter is learning how to reverse the curse of not giving. The secret to receiving is simply giving. Most of us who lack financially are not mature and are not givers. But we must be careful that we are planting the right seed in the right soil. Bad soil produces no harvest.

**Matthew 7:6 "Give not that which is holy unto the dogs, neither cast ye your pearls before swine, lest they trample them under their feet,**

**and turn again and rend you."** Sowing in the right soil is critical. Let me simplify this.

For example, Mary is involved in a very abusive relationship. The man whom she desires treats her badly and continues to disrespect her and tear her self-esteem down. Despite all of this, she still tries to keep the relationship going hoping that some day he may change and become the man of her dreams. She's failing to realize that she's not equally yoked with him. It's important to know that giving to people who don't really appreciate your kindness will set you back mentally, physically and financially.

**Matthew 13:3-9 "And he spake many things unto them in parables, saying, Behold, a sower went forth to sow; 4And when he sowed, some seeds fell by the way side, and the fowls came and devoured them up: 5Some fell upon stony places,**

**where they had not much earth: and forthwith they sprung up, because they had no deepness of earth:**

**6And when the sun was up, they were scorched; and because they had no root, they withered away.
7And some fell among thorns; and the thorns sprung up, and choked
them: 8But other fell into good ground, and brought forth fruit, some an hundredfold, some
sixtyfold, some thirtyfold. 9Who
hath ears to hear let him hear."**

Another critical point is *our words are seeds.* So when we speak we must believe what we say. If we speak and doubt what we said, we kill our harvest.

**Mark 11:24 "Therefore I say to you, whatever things you ask when you pray, believe that you receive them and you shall have them."**

**Proverbs 18:21 "Death and life are in the power of the tongue: and they that love it shall eat the fruit thereof."**

As believers we should be givers, because that's our assignment in this life.

**Romans 12:1 "I beseech you therefore, brethren, by the mercies of God, that ye present your bodies a living sacrifice, holy, acceptable unto God, which is your reasonable service."**

So as true believers we must withstand trials, being rebuked, scorned and lied upon. I know you may say to yourself this doesn't sound good, but when you are kin to the King, it's the Good Life. I hope the principles I laid out in this chapter will be beneficial to you because everything you need is already inside of you and God has many things waiting for you.

**1 Corinthians 2:9 "But as it is written, Eye hath not seen, nor ear heard, neither have entered into the heart of man, the things which God hath prepared for them that love him.**" So I hope you realize that God's word is priceless and free to all mankind.

THE POWER TO GET WEALTH: NO MONEY REQUIRED

## REQUIREMENT

## Chapter Seven

# POWER

Power is the most important principle in this book. Without it, nothing is possible. This chapter is the key to your success and understanding of all the previous chapters. It is very important that this chapter be read with the Christ-like mind, not the 'natural' mind. **Philippians 2:5 "Let this mind be in you, which was also in Christ Jesus."** This chapter was put together without any notes so I hope and pray that God leads my path with wisdom, knowledge, power and revelation.

According to the dictionary the word ***Power*** means ***ability to do or act; capability of doing or accomplishing something.*** When you hear the word Power, what comes to your mind? Most human beings strive to have power whether it's over their lives, their family, their jobs or their vices and temptations. Power can be used in so many different ways. It can be used to help or hurt someone.

Most people don't realize the power they possess. This is especially true in the church. Satan's main goal is to keep the believer from having any Power. God is not looking for who can recite the word; he's looking for who can apply the word. Without power the believer is ineffective in God's kingdom.

In order to activate your spiritual power, it's important to understand and know God's word. Most pastors think that if you confess with your mouth and believe within your heart that Jesus Christ is Lord, you will be saved. This is easier said than done.

That's why we see so many believers go to church every Sunday to worship and praise God, but at their worldly ways on Monday through Sunday confused and disgusted. Notice how loosely we use the word 'saved' as if we have made it or gotten over all of our hurdles in life. If we were all 'saved' there would be no need for a savior (Jesus Christ). It's very important that we understand that we are saved daily by grace. It's an on-going process.

Satan loves when the believer thinks in the natural mind and uses the word saved without understanding. **2 Timothy 1:7 "For God hath not given us the spirit of fear; but of power,**

**and of love, and of a sound mind."** According to the dictionary, the word ***sound*** means ***free from injury, damage, defect, disease; in good condition; healthy; robust.***

A sound mind is a mind that is stayed on God. **Isaiah 26:3 "Thou wilt keep him in perfect peace, whose mind is stayed on thee: because he trusteth in thee."** In order to possess spiritual power you must be in perfect peace, because peace is the absence of confusion and confusion is the absence of peace.

Understanding who God is is essential to activate the power we possess. **John 1:1 "In the beginning was the Word, and the Word was with God, and the Word was God."**

The word is God and the word became flesh. So, who are we? **Genesis 5:1-2 "This is the book of the generations of Adam. In the day that God created man, in the**

**likeness of God made he him; male and female created he them; and blessed them, and called their name Adam, in the day when they were created."**

You are a little god; so everything God created, you can possess. There are no limits to what you can obtain or achieve if you have faith and you believe. **Psalms 82:6 "I have said, ye are gods; and all of you are children of the most high."** You must know this in order to be in God's kingdom and possess his Power. **1 Corinthians 4:20 "For the kingdom of God is not in word, but in power."** We can read the word as well as memorize the scriptures but unless we can put what we read into action it's useless.

It's no different than someone memorizing Martin Luther King Jr's great speeches. They can stand in front of an audience and recite his speeches with passion as well as conviction, but reciting his speeches does not take the place of walking in the shoes that he walked in and accomplishing the things he accomplished through faith and belief. It took power to produce what King produced. It's just like that old saying "*You must walk the walk and talk the talk.*"

For example, a man is sentenced to two years in a state prison for drug possession. Although he's locked up and away from society, he still manages to get drugs inside of the jail. He uses deceptive ways to get drugs in and pays other prisoners to transport the drugs to his cell. It takes power for him to do that.

He devised a plan, acted on it and accomplished his purpose by getting drugs from the outside in for his use. The same person could use his power to set up a plan to get off of drugs and get his life back on track and become a noble citizen.

Satan is a master of deception. He'll motivate us to work towards something wrong and discourage us from doing something right. An idle mind is the devil's workshop. This is why it is important that you have the Christ-like mind and stay focused by speaking the word, doing the word and loving the word.

It is sad to say that most believers go to church every week attending service, listening to what the pastor is saying, taking notes, memorizing scriptures, praising God, rejoicing and celebrating the word; yet lack the ability to overcome many of their problems. This is why the word says in **2 Timothy 3:5 "Having a form of godliness, but denying the power thereof: from such turn away."** We see in this scripture that a believer can have a form of godliness.

According to the dictionary the word ***form*** means ***a particular condition, character, or mode in which something appears***. Satan loves when the believer takes on a form mentality because it's not of God; it's of him. When we act on the word it requires the Power of the Holy Spirit and Satan can't stop the Holy Spirit. **Matthew 26:41 "Watch and pray, that ye enter not into temptation: the spirit indeed is willing, but the flesh is weak."**

The flesh produces nothing and the spirit produces everything. If we deny the Christ-like mind and follow our own mind, we are falling into Satan's trap. It is extremely important that we don't lean on our own understanding. Most believers lack the power of the Holy Spirit because they're given a 'watered-down word' and not the proper understanding of how the spirit works versus the flesh.

It is extremely crucial that the believer understand how the flesh produces nothing but self-centered desires and temptations. **Romans 8:9 "But ye are not in the flesh, but in the Spirit, if so be that the Spirit of God dwell in you. Now if any man have not the Spirit of Christ, he is none of his."**

Satan loves a fleshly believer because they are deceived by self will and not God's will. **Galatians 5:16-17 "This I say then, Walk in the Spirit, and ye shall not fulfill the lust of the flesh. For the flesh lusteth against the Spirit, and the Spirit against the flesh: and these are contrary the one to the other: so that ye cannot do the things that ye would."**

Satan loves a double-minded believer because he knows that the believer can't accomplish anything in God's kingdom. **James 1:8 "A double-minded man is unstable in all his ways."**

This simply means that anyone, whose mind is not stayed on Christ, will be unstable; not in some ways, but all of his ways. You cannot trust or believe that person for what they say or what they do. Their lives will be like a seesaw, up and down. It is sad to say that most church people suffer from these symptoms because they are caught up in a 'feel good' gospel void of power and peace.

The Christ-like mind is the only way to salvation, no exceptions. Once again, Jesus said 'let this mind be in you'. Now we see that it is not about us; it is about him. So it is extremely important that you take yourself out of it and put God first. **Ephesians 2:8 "For by grace are ye saved through faith; and that not of yourselves: it is the gift of God."** When it's his will, it will be your blessing. When it's your will, it will lead to a lesson.

So, to sum this all up, it is not difficult to receive the power of the Holy Spirit. You must be willing to let go and let God and he will direct our paths. **Psalm 37:23 "The steps of a good man are ordered by the LORD: and he delighteth in his way."** There is so much in store for the believer if we live with expectation in the Christ-like mind. If we stay in the spirit and get away from religion we'll be able to live the blessed life.

*Living in the blessing*

We cannot do anything without having God's Holy Spirit and power. The result of having power and a sound mind is a blessed life. Some may say they are blessed. That's correct. We are blessed just to wake up each morning and have a roof over our head and food to eat. Yet, God desires us to live in the blessing, not just to be blessed.

Most Christians do not live in the fullness of the blessing. They are satisfied with crumbs from the enemy's table just like Lazarus was. However, God wants the believer to have more than enough, not just enough, because if you have just enough, you can't be a blessing to others. God's plan for the believer is that we be doers of the word. **James 1:22 "But be ye doers of the word, and not hearers only, deceiving your own selves."** He said that we would be blessed going in and blessed coming out which means favor will be all around you.

He desires more for you, not just a roof over your head, food to eat and a job. We are more than conquerors. We are kin of the King. **Isaiah 45:3 "And I will give thee the treasures of darkness, and hidden riches of secret places, that thou mayest**

**know that I, the LORD, which call thee by thy name, am the God of Israel."** God has so many things waiting for us once we are living in the blessing. This is why faith and expectation are so important. You must believe in order to receive what God has waiting for you.

**Psalm 91:1 "He that dwelleth in the secret place of the most high shall abide under the shadow of the Almighty."** The believer must know that Christ walked through the valley of the shadow of death for us. He has already paid the price. Once you are living in the fullness of the blessing, you are living under the shadow of the almighty. **Romans 8:31 "What shall we then say to these things? If God be for us, who can be against us?"**

Just knowing this should make you jump for joy. Once you get this in your spirit and in your bones no devil in hell can stop you. Blessings begin to overtake you. Trials become just a test for you. Once you receive power, the things that used to hinder you the most becomes easy. **2 Corinthians 5:17 "Therefore if any man be in Christ, he is a new creature: old things are passed away; behold, all things are become new."**

I want you to say to yourself seven times a day. "I am the head and not the tail. I shall lend and not borrow. I have confidence. I have faith. I have knowledge. I have wisdom and I have power."

## The seven keys

**Key 1:** Now that we understand the true meaning of **wealth** which literally means **'all needs met'**, we are secure and confident within ourselves and our abilities.

**Key 2: Self Worth equals Wealth**. We are joint heirs with Christ and more than conquerors; we will look inside of ourselves and draw from all of the gifts that God has already stored inside of us and know that we are already wealthy and that we are the head and not the tail. We are blessed going in and blessed coming out. We have a mind set of expectation.

**Key 3:** Now Faith is. Not tomorrow, but now. We will no longer just touch the hem of his garment we will reach for the top. We will not just have the faith the size of a mustard seed; we will develop the faith the size of a mountain. We will be hearers and doers of the word.

**Key 4:** We are citizens of the **Kingdom.** We will operate like kings and queens and know that the kingdom is to come, not to go. We are highly favored, we are mighty warriors and encouraged believers. We change the atmosphere where ever we go because we are not just blessed; we are living in the blessing.

**Key 5:** Spending time with the word is very important. Relaxing, meditating, letting go, letting God; receiving your **Vision**; making way for your provision; writing down exactly what God has said to you; being patient, obedient and faithful.

**Key 6:** You are valuable and you attract wealth. Remembering that you are favored and that men shall pour into your bosom; having a mind set of expectation; expecting for things to come after you. You shall lend and not borrow. Money comes after you so withdraw out of the bank that God has already stored inside of you. We don't work for money; we tithe, we sow and we reap. We should never use the word spend; we should always use the word invest. Avoid foolish conversations and make sure every move is an investment.

**Key 7:** Reading God's word and applying the principles that were given to you in this book as well as exercising your faith, prayers, vision, belief and obedience will get you in position to receive the **Power** that God already has waiting for you. Once these principles are applied no devil in hell will be able to defeat you.

"Now that I have shared God's word with you about whom you are and whose you are and the power that we possess as believers in the blood of Jesus, there should not be any excuse for you to fail."

###

# ABOUT THE AUTHOR

Keith Douglas was born in Chicago, IL and raised in Los Angeles CA. He knows he has what it takes to make his mark in society. Moving to Los Angeles, he saw where he wanted to take his journey and from there he learned the system at hand. With years of experience and patience, Keith decided to develop his own company with his law partner Joseph Gellman something that will not only speak to the music industry but allow opportunities as well.

From there RKD Music Management was born. He has been in the music and entertainment business for 15 years managing, advising and giving aid to the inquiring and talented minds of today. In addition, he is also responsible for music on the movie 'This Christmas" soundtrack

which released in 2007 with *Chris Brown, Loretta Devine* and *Idris Elba*.
Keith was co- producer of the film "Jada" in 2009 which is now on DVD in stores. The film featured actors *Clifton Powell, Rockmond Dunbar, Sienna Goines* to name a few.

RKD Music & Talent Management has recently launched Speakers Bureau Institute (SBI), an agency catered to actors and musicians providing a platform for speaking engagements and appearances. Keith is a spokesman for many Gospel Conferences. He is Executive Producer of The Book of David: The Transition CD by Dave Hollister which was nominated for a 2007 BET Gospel Album of the Year and was honored for 2009 Stop the Violence "Think Education: Put God First" Award by City of Refuge *Bishop Noel Jones*.

This is Keith's first debut book, titled the ***The Power to Get Wealth: No Money Required.*** "It's a plethora of experiences of my life in this world", says Keith. One empowering quote Keith lives by and shares frequently, "Quitters never win, winners never lose."

KEITH DOUGLAS MINISTRIES

## "So, what's your story?"

I would like to invite you to visit KeithDouglas.org and share your testimony. This website is designed not only as a place to share your stories but also a resource and interaction opportunity to help you fulfill your vision.

**www.keithdouglas.org**

To contact Keith Douglas, write:

Keith Douglas Ministries

P.O. Box 11611

Beverly Hills, CA 90213

*Please include your prayer requests and comments when you write.*